A Limb Outgrowing a Weathered Tree

poems by

Whitnee Coy

Finishing Line Press
Georgetown, Kentucky

A Limb Outgrowing a Weathered Tree

Copyright © 2025 by Whitnee Coy
ISBN 979-8-89990-121-8 First Edition
All rights reserved under International and Pan-American Copyright Conventions. No part of this book may be reproduced in any manner whatsoever without written permission from the publisher, except in the case of brief quotations embodied in critical articles and reviews.

ACKNOWLEDGMENTS

"Lost Bugler Smoke"—*Choeofpleirn Press*
"The Separation"—*The Word's Faire & Alien Buddha Press*
"It's Funny What People Will Say & Do to One Another"—*Here Journal & Alien Buddha Press*
"sadie miller," T*he Word's Faire & Alien Buddha Press*
"Meeting Again"—*Alien Buddha Press*
"How Long Do You Visit?"—*Highland Park Poetry, Daily Poetry Feature & Alien Buddha Press*
"Catching Up" and "a year"—*Cypress Review*

Publisher: Leah Huete de Maines
Editor: Christen Kincaid
Cover Art: Mark Zimmerman, https://greeninkgalleryandstudios.com
Author Photo: Whitnee Coy
Cover Design: Elizabeth Maines McCleavy

Order online: www.finishinglinepress.com
also available on amazon.com

Author inquiries and mail orders:
Finishing Line Press
PO Box 1626
Georgetown, Kentucky 40324
USA

Contents

The Separation 1

Oral History 2

How Long Do You Visit? 3

 Clamoring Outsides 4

It's funny what people will say & do to relate to one another 5

Meeting Again 7

Catching Up 8

a year 10

Settled Reality 11

Lost Bugler Smoke 12

sadie miller 14

for the gentlest love i've ever known: jesse coy.
for the lights of my life: ben, elouise, & sadie miller.

i love you all more than words.

to all those families who have loved a baby in the NICU

The Separation

Before they pulled her wet-slicked being
from my numbed body, they prepped us
we may not hear her cry.

Minutes before, her heart rate dived
to a faint tap & her 3lb body
had stopped moving.

No matter if I had changed position,
sipped chilled water, or however deep
they dug the ultrasound wand into me;

her life-filled body had become lifeless.

As my body rocked back &
forth like a swing in the wind, they carved
through 7 layers of my body.

I shivered from the coldness of metal tools
slicing thick tissue & the nurse to my right
gabbled everything they were doing, reasons why, &

I couldn't hear a thing. Only thoughts of how
my 7-month-old baby that had grown a part of me
may not scream, cry, feel, or be alive.

My husband rested his hand on my hairnet
& soon we heard little bleats, a wet lamb
dropped in a pasture left to survive.

In a moment, we became two entities
left to laugh, wail, & feel the world's aches

separate.

Oral History

years to come
your red hair
will have wisps of silver,
like tinsels icing trees at Christmas
& everything will be a memory

your dad & i
long gone snapshots
childhood floods you
at times, you least
suspect it.

you'll know you
got your dad's eye color
—an ocean clear with sun
sparkling on the riptides.

you'll know you
got my eye shape
—wide, half-dollar sized circles
left on check-out counters
in a Kentucky summer to pay.

you'll remember all
that has been told to you
over the years by those who love you.

mamie's pet spider monkey,
yellow-edged valentine's day cards tucked
in shoe boxes. siblings staggered on ladders
to look over the fence during COVID
nattering with neighbor kids. adoption
papers found & trees passed down to the tribe.
summer cabin camping plans, Rathco concerts,
board games, dogs that never barked,
dogs that always barked, ripped trampoline nets,

the day you were born & we almost died.

How Long Do You Visit?

Her breathing on my chest
sounds like the slow release of a balloon
hissing after months of not
knowing how strong of a breather
she would be.

A hospital stay that long makes you tired
& confused & drifting in realities
where your baby is living outside your body
without you. You produce milk for no
one & days meld together & roll around
like marbles in a mouth.

People always want to know
how long you visit each day.
Like there's a sweet spot of time
that makes you a better mother
or father. The more time
drips by that, you stare into a clear
box watching for chest movements of this baby,
a featherless, fallen bird.
If you say hours, there's an immediate pity
& confusion about how work
is letting you, or how your dishes
aren't sink-stacked, & how are your other kids surviving?
If you say about an hour,
there's a tinge of disgust
& a comment on how they could
never leave their baby
alone.

As if time were a testament to motherhood.
A testament to your womanhood.

Clamoring Outsides

living next to an elementary school
i'd hear the bells clamor
between periods, rushing sweaty-
palmed kids in halls
to math equations, spelling bees,
& recess with broken swings,

as i waited in bed for the daily
doctor's call from the NICU.
*last night was fine, not much
to report, no news is good enough
news, only one episode
where the nurse had to
help her breathe.*

my breast milk was drying
no matter how many images
of the baby or videos I would watch of her
breathing with the help of a machine.
no matter how much fatty food or coconut-filled drinks
or maple-flavored supplements.
no matter how many hours or minutes
or seconds sat next to her clear box
watching her spindles for arms
with IVs, yellow & jaundiced.

the world charged on
outside of my pulled blinds
& the sucks and pulls
of a hospital-used breast pump
on my bedside for 45 days
was all I heard when
nursing a machine.

It's funny what people will say & do to relate to one another

Her purple-hued legs, as long as my fingers
& the tubes that ran throughout her body
were as thick as her pine-needle arms.

When you explain to people
your baby is in the NICU, they never know what to say.
Prattle about a baby they once knew
who survived or read about
in a Facebook post. They preach phrases like "normal,"
"you'd never know," "even graduated early," or
"only had a hole in their heart" to make you feel relieved.
Jostle, how lucky you are & how thankful
you should feel. Your baby will be *fine*, & these moments
will pass when you can't hold her, feed her, bathe her,
touch her petal-thick skin that you once grew.

Curious people ask if her eyesight
will be okay & I wonder if oxygen
lines will snake through her nose forever.
Or pry if she will always be so tiny—can she catch up?
All I can think of is that because she was born
so young, she hadn't learned the reflex of suckling
& swallowing. No matter how many breastfeeding articles I read,
it would never matter as a toothpick-sized orange
feeding tube winds through her nose for nearly 45 days.

It's funny what people will say &
do to relate to one another.

When in the dark of night, while everyone rests
& IVs streak both of your arms, you cry
with no sound, so nurses or your husband don't hear
because you should be thankful you survived.
She survived.
But your body feels empty

& your arms pine to hold her
foot-long body next to yours in rough
patterned hospital sheets.

Instead, in the quiet beeps of hospital rooms
you grieve the dreams you had
for your pregnancy, birth, & the beginning
days of her life.

Grief's like heavy weights
tied to your feet as you learn to walk again,
shuffle one foot after another
to the NICU in the morning light.

Meeting Again

At your dad's track meeting
with his students & their families,
the nurse who cradled me
as I was dying, was there
with her family.

That night, she kept shaking her head
saying she didn't know what to do
questioning why my body
was turning inside out on itself,
after a healthy pregnancy.

She didn't recognize me
months later, as I didn't hold
nearly 30 pounds
of swollen skin, ballooning
as my liver leaked blood.
I wasn't yowling from pain
in urine-soaked bed sheets.

When she hugged me
she held on tight
moving her hand over my shoulder
blades, touching reality.

She rocked my body,
the same way she had that night

willing me to live.

Catching Up

I've never been good
at math, the jumbling of numbers
of any kind, and yet

here I am, mentally subtracting
2.5 months from your actual age
at any given second to discover
your adjusted age—
a concept before you that
I never knew it existed. While you
exist in your actual age, white coats
until the age of two will only see you
as adjusted.

There was a period after you were born
when your doctors didn't even view you
as alive. There was nothing to compare
you to, a developing baby not yet
on its own. How could a baby, supposed to be
still in the womb, develop skills
like breathing and swallowing
10 weeks early? Outside and disconnected
from life and still living?

November 26th, 2023
was supposed to be your birthday
& now on computer-typed forms
& certificates & conversations
or party invitations, it will always say
September 17th, 2023.

Your pediatrician, teary-eyed
thumbed through paperwork
to tell us after months
of tube feedings, syringes of medicine,

IVs, blood test pricks, eye exams
you had made it to the 3rd percentile
of your actual age.

You were finally alive.

a year

nearly 9 months alive
outside of the womb
& you said *mama*
lips pursed like a turtle's
& stood in your playpen
with sunshine radiating
behind your body.

on monday evenings,
when your dad & i share a beer;
a ritual we began between schedules
we rock you in our favorite wooden booth
as you sip 8 ounces of formula
eyes wide, looking at fellow regulars.

you can now wear a red-checked
flannel i wore when i was 7 months old,
yet still wear baby sandals, velcroed straps
made for those at 6 months of age.

5 bodies move through our home
exploding with baby toys, shaving cream slime,
empty dog food bowls, notebooks scribbled
with days of the week, dress-up costumes
of wild west outlaws, scraped-toe cowboy boots
& mud pieces tracked in from garden digs.

belly laughing, deep-voiced at 4 months old,
your 3 favorite furry friends made you
have gummy open-mouth smiles,
your full face shows 2 deep dimples.

in fewer months than i carried you,
you'll be 1 years old exploring a world
not ready for your early existence.

Settled Reality

over 24 hours after she was
sawed from my body,
a limb outgrowing a weathered tree;
I was able to touch her
for the first time.

hands washed, scrubbed with
little plastic-bristle brushes
& a timer ticking away.

she wasn't pressed
wet & purple to my chest
like the movies
or the stories from friends
or the moments I had envisioned
months before. instead buttons
pushed to calibrate oxygen
inside her container & given permission
to slide my fingers nearly the length
of her body, skipping vessels & cords
chartering from her stomach,
nose, arms, and head
keeping her alive. I sat wilted;
a crumpled shell in an open-
backed hospital gown.

to lose something without losing it
can't be explained
but grief settles still the same;

light speckled dust on the top
no matter how much you clean.

Lost Bugler Smoke

I've never seen an adult cry
like how I saw my grandmother
sob into my mother's shoulder,
while clinging to a smoke-filled
quilt, her mother
had made.

That day was long, moving
my grandmother & packing
her home of 19 years. Boxes perched
on shelves, watching us like roosted
owls supervising scampered field mice.
A home emptied into a house
as night overcame the sky
& settled thick
in the Kentucky summer air.

Near midnight,
we found ourselves
surrounding a rusted trunk
in my grandmother's bedroom.
She navigated the crooked
levers, releasing the top. Golden, aged
pillowcases once white
protected precious hand-stitched
quilts. My grandmother sifted
through the colorful blocked canvases
of her mother, & of a time
when she was still alive. Twisted yarn poked
through each design, reflecting an Appalachian
way to quilt; hand tying.

In minutes, what smelled like a fire
burned our noses & filled the room
with haze. The three of us peered around
wondering what was happening, as the room
filled with fog.

My grandmother
released her voice like an animal
caught in a trap, "*It's her. It's her cigarette
smoke. I've opened the trunk
& I'm losing her.*" The trunk's top
slammed shut in between her inconsolable cries.
My great-grandmother's Bugler
tobacco smoke had filled the room,
seeping off the heirlooms released
from the opened trunk. My grandmother's
shoulders hunched, & her spine
poked through her shirt
with each earth-pulling cry.

Her wails, nothing that I had heard
& my own mother rocked her,
a boat trying to ride rough waves
through a storm. Soon, they both stood still,
& what sounded like the breaking
of bodies silenced in the haze.

We don't always know; the emptiness
that resides in a body not our own—no matter
how much we love & think we know.

We don't always know what will break us open.

sadie miller,

you were named within an hour
on a cross-country road trip
as your dad zipped us
back from kentucky to south dakota,
a state i swore i would never return to.

things change & minds can change too
    //remember that when moments get hard &
    you worry about what happens
    if you learn more or grow & new possibilities
    look as sweet as blackberries
    try them//

on december 8th i knew things would never
be the same as i sat across from your dad
laughing so deep, i never felt more alive
or more like myself. every fear i knew
crumbled like dry leaves beneath feet.

    now watching you,
nearly 11 pounds at 5 months old,
you laugh fully. mouth extending,
showing mountains of pink gums.
dimples rippling over the pond of your face
    //always laugh fully, letting it take over the room
    filling up spaces not originally made for you
    but you built for yourself//

your siblings cradled you
when they themselves were nothing but children,
& prayed your little 3-pound body
would live through the night your heartbeat
dropped. they practiced consoling their cousin's
baby dolls to be the best for you
    //love B & E always
    they will always be there for you//

don't forget that 912 franklin, our home,
is made of board games, art-lined walls, spilled
sodas, zach bryan crooning records, kisses,
& pizza crusts left for dogs to eat.
it's muddy socks from trampoline jumps,
the best you can do on homework, heavy-gripped
hugs & hands held on couches piled with
extra blankets. there's always time
for naps, late-night television shows, belly laughter,
paint brushes left unclean, noah kahan stick-poke
tattoos, cat meows, stories of won recess-superbowls,
broken drumsticks, opened books, solved
math equations, empty drawn-on coffee mugs
& everything
in between.

> //remember, the best is found in the quietest of moments
> & times that feel messy. remember that love isn't linear
> or comes when you want it, but instead, at times, you need it.
>
> remember, you are the best of us we could offer
> & it still won't be enough for you//

Whitnee Coy is an award-winning writer and educator, living in the Black Hills of South Dakota with her husband, Jesse, and their 3 kids. She was raised by her single mother and grandmother in Lexington, KY, where she attended the School for the Creative and Performing Arts (SCAPA) for Creative Writing and the KY Governor's School for the Arts. Whitnee has her MFA in Creative Writing from Eastern Kentucky University's Bluegrass Writers Studio and has three collections of poetry published including *this deep, wide, dark world* (Alien Buddha Press). She has recently published the social-emotional learning children's book, *Elsie's Adventures to Brainy Cove* exploring topics of the neuroscience behind emotions and coping skills for emotional regulation that can be done at home or in school. She is finishing her doctorate in Education Policy, Organization, and Leadership with an emphasis in Diversity and Equity. She is a professor at Oglala Lakota College on the Pine Ridge Reservation and when she isn't working or writing she loves spending time with her husband and family.

www.ingramcontent.com/pod-product-compliance
Lightning Source LLC
Chambersburg PA
CBHW022110080426
42734CB00009B/1542